GODS OF INDIA

Brahma's Wise Boons

SHUBHA VILAS

Brahma is the Creator in the Holy Trinity. The Universe we live in is also created by him. In fact, Brahmadeva is considered the grandfather of all living beings. That's because he had the responsibility of creating not only the Universe but also all the living beings within it.

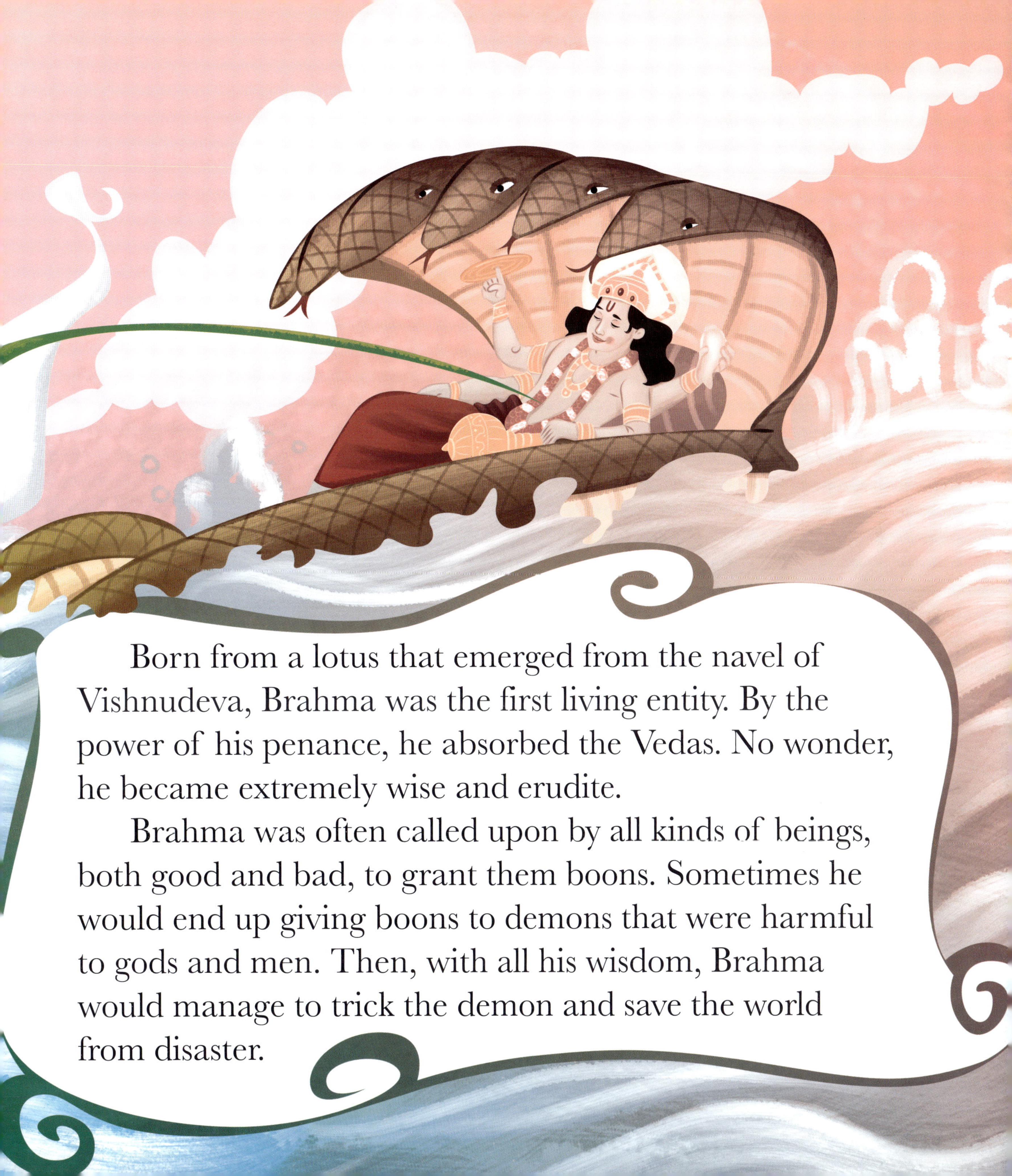

Born from a lotus that emerged from the navel of Vishnudeva, Brahma was the first living entity. By the power of his penance, he absorbed the Vedas. No wonder, he became extremely wise and erudite.

Brahma was often called upon by all kinds of beings, both good and bad, to grant them boons. Sometimes he would end up giving boons to demons that were harmful to gods and men. Then, with all his wisdom, Brahma would manage to trick the demon and save the world from disaster.

One day, he was in samadhi when he felt a great force pulling him towards the Earth. Someone was desperately praying and meditating for a boon. He could never be sure what the demand would be and what he would be compelled to give.

Soon, he found himself in front of Ravana, the king of Lanka. Worse, he was not alone, but with his demonic brothers and sister.

Bracing himself, Brahma gently told Ravana to stop the severe austerities he was performing and ask for a boon.

Indeed, Ravana had been indulging in intense practice by cutting off his nine heads and offering them to Brahmadeva. As soon as Brahma touched him, all his heads reappeared.

Ravana had been eagerly waiting for this day. Given that Brahma was related to him as his great-grandfather, he would definitely grant him all the boons.

‘I want to become immortal,’ Ravana demanded greedily. He was already thinking of how he would conquer the Universe if he became deathless.

Brahma shook his head, ‘No son, I cannot grant you that because whoever is born has to die.

Ravana then asked for a boon that he could not be killed by any god,gandharva, yaksha or any other celestial being. Lord Brahma granted him the nectar of immortality which he placed in Ravana's navel.

Now he could not be defeated by yakshas, gods, wild beasts, gandharvas, devas, asuras, nagas, birds. To Ravana, humans posed no threat to his life whatsoever, so they were not part of the boon. Wise Brahma knew what Ravana was assuming. He smiled. He knew that Ravana would meet his end at the hands of Lord Rama who would be born as a human!

Next, Brahma turned to Kumbhakarana. Knowing well that another such demand was on the way, Brahma silently communicated with Saraswatidevi, goddess of knowledge, to manipulate the words of Kumbhakarana.

Saraswati swiftly sat on Kumbhakarana's tongue and when Kumbhakarana asked for 'Indra-asan' (throne of Indra), she made it sound like 'Nidra-asan' (throne of sleep). While Brahma was delighted to grant him lifelong sleep and save the world, Kumbhakarana went into a frenzy. He cried piteously explaining this was not what he wanted.

Finally, Brahma took pity on him and modified the boon so that he would sleep for six months and be awake for a day and then sleep again for six months. This boon also reduced the power and might of the greedy Kumbhakarana.

Now it was Vibhishana's turn. Although he was Ravana and Kumbhakarana's brother, he had no demonic desires. In fact, he was a devotee of Sri Rama and asked for lifelong devotion for his Supreme God and a life guided by dharma.

Brahma beamed with joy. This was the kind of boon he loved to bestow. Love for God and righteousness. Not power and wealth that everyone seemed to be wanting. Brahma not only granted him unwavering love for Sri Rama but he also added a bonus –an eternal life. In this way, Vibhishana became immortal.

Lastly, Brahma asked Surpanakha, Ravana's ugly sister what she wanted. Since Surpanakha was only focussed on outer beauty, she appealed to him to give her the power to change her appearance as per her wish. Brahma thought it was harmless enough and said, 'Tathastu.' Without wasting a moment, Brahma left from the scene, afraid that they would want more from him if he stayed there longer.

Thus we see that when demons try to take advantage of his kindness, Brahma manages to manipulate the most complicated boons to the advantage and relief of human beings.

Brahma is the chief deity of the Pushkar temple in Rajasthan. The sanctum sanctorum of this ancient temple holds the image of the four-headed Brahma and his consort Gayatri (goddess of the Vedas).

On Kartik Poornima, a large number of pilgrims visit the temple after bathing in the sacred Pushkar lake to celebrate the festival dedicated exclusively to Brahma.